In a Poetic Mood

Poems for children

Sanmeet Kaur Sarna

ISBN 978-93-5610-126-5
© Sanmeet Kaur Sarna 2022
Published in India 2022 by Pencil

A brand of
One Point Six Technologies Pvt. Ltd.
123, Building J2, Shram Seva Premises,
Wadala Truck Terminal, Wadala (E)
Mumbai 400037, Maharashtra, INDIA
E connect@thepencilapp.com
W www.thepencilapp.com

DISCLAIMER: *The opinions expressed in this book are those of the authors and do not purport to reflect the views of the Publisher.*

Author biography

Sanmeet Kaur Sarna has been writing poems ever since a kid. She says poetry is the best way of expressing ones emotions and feelings. She has completed her education from Bundelkhand University and has eight years of experience in teaching. Other than writing poems she is also very fond of listening english music.

This book is a collection of poems written for the kids who are a poetry lover and seek for inspiration through poetry.

CONTENTS

Introduction

Here is a collection of poems, written in simple language and can be understood easily. These poems impart knowledge to the readers. The rhyming used in these poems make them interesting and worth reading. This collection of poems is specially for children who enjoy reading poem.

In a Poetic Mood

Happiness

Happiness is like spring
It never stays for long

The moment we start enjoying it
We realise it's gone.
What's left behind is fragrance
Of some sweet memories
And a smile as a parting gift
With promises to keep.

So before it's too late
Let's learn to enjoy
  Don't worry about the future
Or the days gone by.
Just focus on your present
Share happiness and try
By sharing blissful moments
Your happiness will multiply.

Cheers to Euphoria

Nestled deep to where I keep
Those memories as souvenirs
Amidst grief, when sorrow tweets
I don't give up or cry.
I rather think about the time
When bliss accompanied
For sake of those blissful moments
I will continue to thrive.

I'll make it through and swim across
Those harsh currents and cold winds
For life, I've learnt is meaningless
 Without pain and tears.
So often when hardships greet
I smile at it and say aloud
Let's meet and part with no regrets
And raise a toast to cheer.

I preserve and treasure well
Each moment of euphoria
So life when takes uneasy turns
I get through alive.
And this is how I've learned to live
No matter whatever I face
I accept every day as a new challenge
And a new beginning in life.

Sunflowers

Fields have been blessed again
With heavy showers of rain
Once again they bloom
To spread across a vibe.
With colours so vibrant
Together when they swing
They sometimes move left
And sometimes towards their right.

In silence as I walk through
Each of them in turn
Gazing at the sky
Where the sun shines bright.
As I observe their faces
Their innocence agreed
In that very moment
Rejuvenates my eyes.

In synch with the cool breeze
A symphony is played
Buzzing in the morning
When creeps in the light.
I follow their leads now
And throughout the day
I enjoy the company
Of bees and butterflies .

Sounds

I hear so many sounds wherever I go
Wings always flutter,
I guess you all know.
What's with the bell
They jingle so well
Heard the whistle of an engine
that's running slow.

I hear so many sounds wherever I go
The chirping of the birds and
Slamming of the door.
Rumbling of the thunder
Whenever it rains
Cheer for the players when they play
their games.

I hear so many sounds wherever I go
The murmur of the music and
the ringing of the phone.
Splash of water
Through TV a roar
If lost in the jungle
There's more to explore.

Through streets of the city,
I hear a sound
Cry of the baby when no one's around.
The clock says tick tock
Now it's time for bed
Close your eyes and sleep
So by morning you feel fresh.

Mother

M stands for magic sprinkled by her hands
O is for the occasion where none but she will give us strength
T stands for her touch that comforts a child's soul
H is for the hope that she gives us when we lose it all
E stands for epic tales we get to hear from her
R is for the reason why we need a mother.

Oh! I Wish

Oh! I wish to be the one
Who flutters all around the flowers
With colourful and spotted wings
I'd fly to where the tulips are
And until they bloom,

Oh Spring!
I promise them a warm embrace
For beauty that you bring along
As a butterfly I'm sure to chase.

Oh! I wish to be the one
Who eagerly the flowers await
So desperate to fly along
With Robins as they migrate
And until they stay
Oh! Spring
I promise them with all my heart
Their little ones they'd take along
 Will treasure all your sweet regards.

When The Sun Sets

Look the sky there above
Revealing that it's nearly time
The sun whispers a goodbye
And calls upon the stars to shine.

Tinted shades of orange and red

Captivates each of us
The crimson hue enhances the view,
When clouds around get a colorful touch.

As colors stretch far and wide
The cloudy sky announces, "It's here"
Dusk along with the moonlight, says
 "Sky looks great when stars appear".

Returning home one and all
The birds are back to cozy nest
As the night begins to roll,
All tired soul needs some rest.

Beautiful

You know what makes you weak
You know what gives you strength
You know your flaws indeed
You have the power to sense.
Don't let nobody judge
No one can criticise
As all of us hold
A heart so beautiful inside.

You know what really hurts
You know what brings in joy
You know yourself so well
You can't really deny.
Don't let nobody judge
No one can criticise
As all of us hold
A heart so beautiful inside.

You Matter

Some of us are like pretty butterflies
Some of us are stars
So beautiful
Some of us have glow
To show the world some light
Some of us have vibes
So natural.

Some of us are strong
Can stand against storm
Some of us can do
What's impossible
Some of us are like
Born to achieve heights
Some of us have strength
To make everything possible.

Some of us are warm
For those went cold
Some of us are loud
So audible
Some of us are streams
 Rejuvinating dreams
Some of us are so strong
and capable.

Isn't it true
All of us have
Some qualities unique
As all of us are rare.
So hold on to yourself
Don't give up or drown
As you matter the most
Don't let yourself down.

A Letter to Santa

I wrote a letter to
Santa not one but two
Bring presents of your own choice

I do enjoy surprise.
If you think two are few
Third one I'll add on to,
Something I'd really like
It would be really nice.

I know you've got a bag
Big enough so I guess
Three won't just fill it up
Do put in some more stuff.
Get me some candies too
Hurry I'll wait for you
On your way do collect
Some more gifts if you get.

I'll leave the door open
For you to tiptoe in
While I'm all lost in dreams
Fill up my Christmas stockings.
I've left them hanging there
You know exactly where.
Sure you will be pleased to see
My beautiful Christmas tree.

Home Sweet Home

Cattles get a shed to live
While grasslands are for deers

Dogs get their own kennel
By water quack - quack sound we hear.

Bunnies live inside a burrow
Cats get a cage.
Kittens stay around their mother
Till they grow up and learn to chase.

Horses live inside a stable
Sheep is found in pen
Hear the roar of lions through the jungle
Where they live in a den.

Animals do need a shelter
They do need a room
A place to live with their loved ones
A home sweet home.

Shades of Spring

Oh! you've got it all
Red, white and blue
Flowers dressed up in pink
And some in orange too.
With colours blooming in
Me as a butterfly
All colours that you bring
I truly enjoy.

Oh! you've got it all
Valleys, plains and hills
All covered up again
With flowers like daffodils.
With colours blooming in
Me as a butterfly
All shades of flowers in spring
I truly enjoy it.

Little Sam

Hey little Sam
Look at the stars,
Shining in the sky.
Can you count all of them,
Or at least try.
Sam cleverly said
Oh, dear!
Those stars are certainly far,
And why are they all
 scattered around,
Ratter being in a jar?
If only they had been together,
All in one place
I would have counted each of them,
without any mistake.

Hey little Sam
Look at the stream,
Flowing down in speed.
Can you count the fishes dear,
Swimming into it?
Sam cleverly said
Oh, dear!
Those fishes in hurry
 Forgot to move in a queue,
And so I worry.
If only they all had been
In a proper line
I'm sure I would have counted them
Without mistake this time.

Success

It's naturally yours and even mine
Success awaits for us this time
Don't wait for night to seek for stars
When we ourselves are born to shine.

Colours

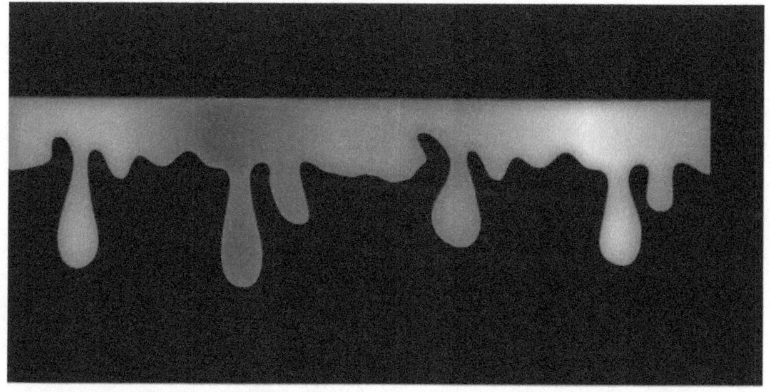

With purple, blue, pink and white
I'll paint you all from head to toe.
No matter who or where you're from
This festive season we will glow.

With orange, red, grey and green
I'll mix them well just to show.
Hand in hand if we walk
Together we are good to go.

With yellow, brown, peach and plum

I'll give you all a gift of smile.
Let's stand against the evil and
Together walk a million miles.

In the Jungle

Trees talk:
The tall trees said to the little plant

"It's a journey so difficult
Oh! little one,
You're so unsafe.

All alone it's hard to grow
Surviving here needs courage.
The fittest win and makes it through
So look at us with a stronger fate
Eventually, you'll disappear
Your weak stems won't bear your weight."

The little one replied

" I know I'm small
A little weak
But even then I'd say I'm brave.
A hope within to survive,
Will help me to grow instead.

Rays of sun and drops of rain,
When poured upon,
I'll get to live
And one day I will grow
As tall as you all did."

"I'll never lose against the storms
Or heavy showers
And day by day,
I challenge you
Keep watching me
I will grow a little bit everyday
Until I become strong."

The Octopus

I live in the ocean blue
Hopefully you know me too
Hey I'm smart and intelligent
I've even got some super sense.

I've got no bones I'm flexible
I can squeeze myself to fit in well
With eight big arms and three hearts
I know the trick of camouflage.

Coral reefs and sea beds
I reside in abyssal depths
I'm fond of clams and even shrimps
Lobsters too I'll put them in.

My tentacles are way too strong
I boss around to save my home
My territory is all I need
To feel secure and freely breathe.

Dreams

When dreams don't come to you
Just go and look for them
Hear them calling you
As the night begins.
Keep some of them in eyes
Before you go to sleep
And stars again tonight
Will make you fall asleep.

Hope

When there's darkness all around
And you're left alone

If you still hope for the best
Night won't be that long.
Sun will rise again
To warm up your heart
Don't give up hope
As darkness never lasts.

Lockdown

Whatever we do,
However we react
But staying in is for our best.
Lets give some time to our own house
That often complains of being left out.

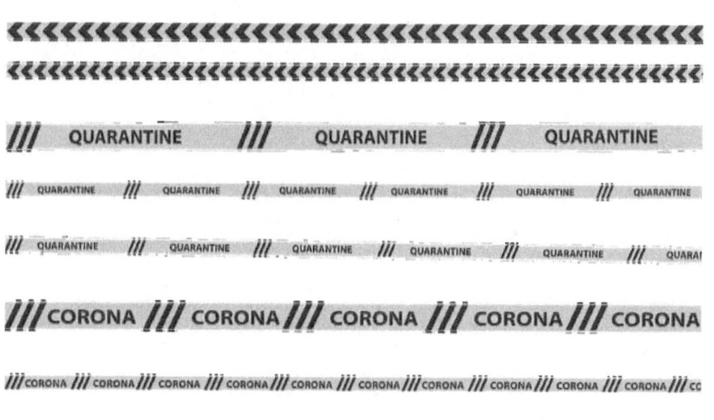

Lets take a look at those four walls
They await for new decor,
And what about the garden, hey
A little change is needed there.
Lets take a look at some old pics,
And reminisce what we have missed.

This time I have a list of things
That I will do while staying in.
I'll watch the stars every night
And so you can, until they hide.
A change is must for everyone
Make memories with your loved ones.
So stay safe, stay home and save lives.
The need of hour, is to stay inside.

Monsoon

Monsoon can come early
Monsoon can be late.
Sometimes it can thrill us
Not everytime I guess.
Scarcity of water
At places flood is faced
Unpredictable are showers
That monsoon brings with it.

Childhood Friend and Memories

There are these moments
Which often connects
You and me forever in life.
Those busy streets and dusty roads
Will always be there to serve as a guide.

While taking me back as I recall
I suddenly feel in butterflies.
Oh! In the past those cricket fields
Still are the same with fimilar vibes.
Outskirts again not really have changed
Those daffodils bloom even today
And as I recall you, My dear friend
I still have a lot to say everyday.
Remember the time when we were young,
We had a bond unbreakable
But time, as they say flies away
And so are we, now poles apart.

Moon- From Crescent To Round

Eerily quiet with crescent white
Holding it so firm
Night along with stars intact
Is likely to be young.

Dwells in deep as time elapse
More or less it's like
A quarter to before it's full

Still shining through the night.

Floats along wee hours of dawn
And finally around
A magic spell I can tell
Weaves it back to round.